Tender Geometries

Mark Dickinson

Tender Geometries

Shearsman Books

First published in the United Kingdom in 2015 by
Shearsman Books
50 Westons Hill Drive
Emersons Green
BRISTOL
BS16 7DF

Shearsman Books Ltd Registered Office
30–31 St. James Place, Mangotsfield, Bristol BS16 9JB
(this address not for correspondence)

www.shearsman.com

ISBN 978-1-84861-335-5

Acknowledgements

My grateful thanks to *Tears in the Fence* for presenting an extract from 'The Tangles'.

Peter Larkin for his guidance, support & friendship. Edric Mesmer for his patience & friendship. And these individuals which along the way I've needed more than they might otherwise know: Matthew Hall, Wendy Mulford, Harriet Tarlo, Amy Cutler, Candice Ward & O. T. Banks. To Eiza, Nemina, Sally & Ann x. And of course to Tony Frazer for all his fabulous work

Contents

Sentinel-Stone

‘But what does it mean to live with the fantasy of commitment, to refuse to receive it according to the prescription of your local lyric poet, and how is *living with it* felt and experienced in language, and what has living with the fantasy and not the reality of commitment meant for a political culture remarkable for mass ‘public’ opposition to the wars prosecuted by their states, and how does duration find its place in poetic language, and can it, like momentariness, be thrilling?’

—Daniel Hayward

‘My poems are my Northern salt, left by a common river, only a gesture rather than a barter because obviously insufficient.’

—Douglas Oliver

‘The poets here may be accused of betraying their class in adopting a “higher” manner, but they also served the dual purpose of bringing “polite” poetry within the grasp of their own native public by relating it to their own places and experience, and of showing that this kind of poetry was not a prerogative of the upper classes, but that the underlings were perfectly capable of grasping its technique and content, and employing it for their own purposes.’

—Peter Riley

‘I am going to replace the subject of “cow” with “child”, in order to reply to your statement/question that: “it’s better to wear the skin off a dead child than to go and kill the child yourself.”’

—Coral Hull

‘It begged for a sentry at that crossing, an honourable
Dissembler standing between civic disgrace and a tithe
Gone white in the sun’

—Andrea Brady

‘A Raven bundled itself into air from midfield
And slid away under hard glistenings, low and guilty’

—Ted Hughes

For E M

Open between the strings of language   rivulets of the gift horizon   where
we are not   written to the letter   between this state & that openness the
vague estuaries leafing through remembrance   strands of a living

Seated   beneath the stars   relinquishing   dreams   of a memory
to breathe   the changing light   or seal   before distinctions
approach   derive   the natural   & settle   within

the amphitheatre   of a superstructure   applying the solution of time
to the morning   hid/den   within the harmony   of imperfect
constitution   waiting passively   for regularities

as the sun   pleats the byres   Never fully reconciled   this human
that natural   centripetal faith   breaking apart   the earth   for a
fresh   field   of the sky   linked   by day

spent   in the slightly nestled footings of faith
wild   desolate   influence   recuperating in the mid
day sun   /dark

emblem Raven   personifies totemic   god   scarce upon the open   sky
the categories of language   fed   fleeting   felt   of lovers
in the narrows of contact

on field & sea   in towns & parks   an open stick   with a vertical crown
O'   corvus   Centrifugal from the reasoning mind
(resident in pairs of life)   the mythic tread of earth   seeding

the ground   in the delicate approach   where the conflict of dialogue
within the coherent scheme of a visible body   becomes sensually draped
within the curves   Where a hand tenders the button   the small cogs

turn   at the time of conversion   the close of palms   fingers   the folding
sky   nests   defines a house   of risen earth   to the upper   vaults
horizontal from the body   the ground   to the surface of the sea

& the daily variations of the innumerable sketch   where symptomatic
intellect abstracts a copy faint within the strata of cloud   like an on-going
bridge   between relations   of the habitable   visible

& measurable   number of the world   A Raven
struck to the totem of god   drilling the whole of origin with a dark edge of
wildness beneath the steel hull of an arc   swerving the desolate

breech   of un calculable horror   settling within the geometrics of
disseminated images   in the form of a forklift   cleft under the anvil
with all the fetish   fingers   onslaught in a choice of form   cast as

expiration   ends meta passage   opens   they call across so not to close
upon   to bridge   with in-
finitely many   scanning the source of what floats on by the sea   trailing

behind its mystery for invisible structures petrified as the fearful course
these are the currents of sound   the close of water   horizoning   hauled
before arrangement   below the threshold   prior to all

this fuss between boredom and confusion measuring and counting
   between one and two   the sensually given object
   between the tread of thought   the serial growth uncertain

linked by day   the field in its rush to be completed   as if
this box   a portion of happiness   or a riot of what we miss   the dialogue
waning not remembering which   as if this matters   falling

upon the ground   staging breath staging expiration   before a small haloed
sunset   flattening horizon   in a long reach toward   the con-vex form of a
cloud   in the brilliant curve of colour   shaping radius

folding a mirror   the surface   baptismal   by what folds into the act
as registers of epoch   or dance   by way of a dream   against
the out-world holding the steer   which bolts

from the very thing we came for   which is   we are remembering
together   beside the track   beside the seaside   this cone   the
architect   the number   & geometry   primed to the whole   small

fingers wrapped around   staring intent at the loss of flavour   declaring
a truth   of luxury   functioning a song   of loss   & remembrance
sticky like toffee apples   tree clumps in farms & parks

all these bind   neglect   tethered to history   salt   fields & sea   fingers
around   a purpose   of class   dis/ located   declaring
less   Raven   you   are the god among

the rabble   of pebbles   I   need   you   picking among the bones
I supply a ticket   I have a purpose   this fork lift truck and all the naked
bodies   Raven   you are mythic like a paper-

weight   you're legitimate   black   with feint metal   figuring me
among the stony cast of walls   Can I speak anymore   "Krahh Krahh"
crying the desolate   or the folds of yellow

Can I say   with a centre and draw an arc forming a moon
in the square root of progression   do I know   or should I settle
in up   lands or coastal cliffs   singing my territory?

Helping my rioting friends because we feel like nothing so fight to feel like
something Raven is it here now is this the morning or just
another mornings flight into the plastic universe where I

would have to Dis agree mining the natural with abandoned
forms still forming folding into each fold of willing choice still
measuring the cut of each fault in the unity of fold upon fold how

many types settle around this place you whisper your whisper & that
laugh so solemn shall we press into each other's otherness
twisting types shall we ripple across our own exactitude enacting

the fraying rights this pass of age transfigures this passage so many
times a square in a circle the I and the N of the dwelling I am not sure
about the stars but that's the milky Way & that's a home

the flower so delicate & I know it's strong the wind opening up
each passage of wings exfoliating mnemonic how these tern so many
ways of going over each scarce trails belonging

where we are folding in to pockets of warmth spoons into the fold of
each other fed beneath these beds of stone and is this love calling through
the seams pressing avenues of slight sealing the earth into

cell the truth marks form within the veil of a radius
sprung to strike heaven this avenue that root before what's taken
embodying minerals embalming skin to breath and breathe

the strain of song each stitch folding the story remember
how it opened the song and how each note pleased your ears where you
listening Raven high above the pylon

did the song I sung reach   or no   is this the penultimate hour before the act
of this forklift truck piles high some bones   is this the excavated tomb or
just some

earth mound or tumulus   under the heavy swell of cumulous   foraging
shells   heaven between the culpable and the responsible   god   so close
beside   the blushing act   beside the coil inserted

in the dark flow   of a quadrant   the facets of all these di-
mentions of facts   but what are you the seer before this act and the next
gravity is not weak   it holds together your numbers

the prime origin   the odd word   spreading out
recalling a stone and an
ancient dyke   with boundaries that can't be seen

from space   Raven   will you return this song to the
under/   world   is the mantle open or does it have a code   elicit me to
carry forth the joy of lapping   where the birds will not be still

enough   where the camera is not good   enough   I dream   of a lens
so that I too can see   into your eyes   Raven   do
you recognise me   in the corridor   between seas

oceans rise   is this the swell of dreaming   or so many seconds
of time and the intervals of space   should I whittle down the mythic lay
cold anti or gaudily wrap myself in the skin of muslin   titillating

my feminine wiles in the wild   anal &
free   in this the cover of earth   a shallow hole of lying   & all those
sheep   the dead and swelling   /small keys beside the intervals

of stone   you have found me   building from the ground up   this is stone
this word   these strings   these are stones   and this
is earth   look at the water   it weighs less than hydrogen and two

of oxygen   the light   the photons without mass   the light   aslant the
window lit   in the circular corridors of the wild   swallowing all the light of
the world   as a hole in the dark   feeding

on the energy of stars   a messenger of mass   reading blocks symmetrically
over the plumes of orbit   comets of water welling of rock   remembering
the water   so many times   un surfacing the solid

frames of   pressing   through darkening skies   rhythms
of neglect   the child peeking through the cosmos   among
the memory of shells   the white sand remembers where the black

Raven cleaves to opportunity   until the dark becomes   an opportunity
beneath those heavy stars   small grains   residues   transits of flight
circling above   is this the wheel of articulation   folding bed upon bed

by shear of mud-stone erf   stone upon stone of site   wherein the field
gathers the shape of things   circular cut slight in the open-right stone   cairn
to guide you home   safe from the body of disruptive waters

old among the mud   clay between stone   stone between clay   bedding the
infill down so that stone will stand as the shelter   where we press down
hard against stone   or warm before stone   lay under between

the earth of sky and the earth of ground   a roof of stone
where earth returns to the niche of stone   and grass grows between the
flags of stone   you can only bed this down   you can only chisel

each sound from the sound of stone   the chisel   hard against the black
stone beak   stone Raven   fingers of fluvial   chiselling
an end   stretched   from the beginning   mineral upon mineral

star upon star   against the body of the moon and a tender hand parting
the way
falling   dark   trailing white   Raven calling

distending   the iris   chiselling the delicate   ply   of skin   as an
opportunistic   forager   on an interwoven structure   set against this
forklift truck   wrote

"shame"   peering   not less   this small insurgent vial   are you
with me Raven   exploring abuse   ash grey   *unprocessed*
and without a number   can we speak of this   or is there another *crisis*

there are words I cannot use   humiliations   without a softness
to touch upon   bent   trauma   am I able to placate you with
sweetness?

Or make a service more palatable with this white & odourless crystalline
powder? Will you take these letters ($C_{12}H_{22}O_{11}$) these numbers that denial
cannot unroll? Speechless without dereliction   interrogates

where imperfect authorised   Raven   but no less than   *in the land*
of loneliness? Beyond the door   there came a door   calling   for the sick
ones   to the sleeping ground

among   placed   rocks   descendents of the buried
casting after the sea   one door and no   windows   made
any grave   breach   a very difficult place   *amongst a few bad*

apples? Alights higher and higher polished so brightly
growing wings in a thousand bright rooms Raven I am in error
tearful among all this stone never accountable love and all of our

ours comprise a family & profitable commodities in the areas we
populate like snails and spiders have blue blood due sounding the
gut like "TTAGGG"[1] and attachments you can't handle

<u>thevisibilityofthecodeisunderlinedinblue</u> and all that matters why?
Not because the wings are black the visible claws the caesura
and usury taps at the door "Oh, no, oh, no!" beautiful white

black dark and lovely rumbling along it's not disinterest nor play
the enchanter <u>itsall thisunderlyingblue</u> attaching itself like meta-lesions
to sweeten at multipoint attachments against the bitterness

of a lower detection threshold for either the protectionist or
the abolitionist longing to talk *wouldn't you like a wishing chair?*
Or is this a matter for applied ethics?

I'm uncertain of poetry when the system functions poorly & creates
uncertainty among the weathered wings of spirit and memory 西王母
(mother

---

[1] The gated line of the wire
Threads succession
And all that strands,

Grooves by tracing spaces,
Grafted in helical fashion
Gift, bonding between the edges.

of the west)   beneath heaven   among the three fold worlds
and many directions   a *place of ravens*   leading from belief
in the recent past   claiming the lives   of people in a day

defending a territory   as *"unkindness"* and *"conspiracy"*   mis-
direct   a flock   mating for life   and all this   treading
quietly   coming along the field to the *stan stane*   out marker

to the sun   by the Loch of Gretchen   through which you
can peep   dancing   as the light steps out
so many shapes stand   politely forgetting   beyond the door

another   its Three-axis form   a RAVEN   mounts   infantry
& supports   CROWS eye-field   to a cloud   burst   of
agony   among   this weathering stone   like rennet

of the slaughtered young   sliced into pieces   "Oh look!"   she cried,
"there's our   1 gram of extract"   *and gave a creak*   to secretly observe
nailing the words together   *a pretty pink cake*   (stunning with electric

current)   & quietly waited   in the open field
("magick")   metal wave guide   across a SOFAR layer in the ocean…

SOUND BENEATH
THE CRESTS
POURING WITH RAIN

***

NEVER AS HAPPY
NOR DEPEND ON
AND ALL OUR

***

SORROW BLUNTS
LIKE ISOLATION
SLOW & DEFICIENT

***

(GASP!)
ENCOMPASSING
THE LAND

f o r   a l l   t h e   t a n g l e s   l a y

N-acetylglucosamine

stray along the sunk

carapace

With a porthole

twist against each other by angles

treads the mark by sound

sites by ebb

f
a
l
l
b
e
un
a
t
h

under log tangles

the tangles

e
a
r
t
s
t
r
y

houses the sink of structure

lays out a word quietly grained

strays a course vested in patience

The Tangles

'Wrecks omit the ambiguity of depth'
—Wendy Mulford

'And white-plummed riders shoreward go

and

THE BIRDS DECLARE IT'
—David Jones

'And drowns the song'
—George Herbert

'They fought with God's cold—
And they could not and fell to the deck
(Crushed them) or water (and drowned them) or rolled
With the sea-romp over the wreck.'
—G. M. Hopkins

'I say this in
Danger aboard our dauncing boat
Hope is a stern purpose'
—J H Prynne

Stretchers knot the tangle, palming night,
midnights strand between the straying

curve of sheet,
as tangles through the histories fade

between the intervals
straining the shell

the sweep of inlet
upon a tangle seals

knots a rate
along a sting lash
between a swash
of each shores salvage

discarding the luminous
amongst a shore of problematic beauty

to which the sea
is lunar seal

by which we abandon
all the crews immunity,
the thump and gnaw
heard beneath the ocean

spoken in drift
carved upon a token
grabbing and heaving
this handful of mess

where nothing
empties
into rain
all nub, the tangles well.

Light

All these hungry voices aching

Found among the seas of grass

The words: *my/ life*

And the scope of water

Discovered in the narrows

Withheld in sand

Approaching an inclement of sky

Held within a curve of grain

& the quadrant of wire

Awash!   Upon a sore

Pre-empting the shores

Horizon   among the shadows

Of Nylon

Seal the mythic with a character of trade where sentences debate pockets of tangles on a shore.

Set incline besets the catalogue of jettisons where sorrowful lines of nylon tangle.

For all sweeps of eider
The shores felt
Sanderling
Across sites of a winter
Light

For the mark as crisp as the sound, laying a bed of grains to granulate duration between a pause:

Hushing the wish, to open whole between un-wanting, to let it flare against a balk of quadrant appraising the route of going to entangle.

Sear the wader
Lightfoot   narrow

Tern

A parting
Accuracy

Volt

A passage
Swift   for occasion

So much particular rots back ingress, not our going but the seething
lit that peels down narrows across the vaulted rib of the stars
(degrees above horizon

Where a fix of the intersection impales upon the tangle, nylons choke holds it limp

Aggravating the very thing we came upon. Gleaned among the long-shores narrow where the crews' endemic way arcs along the partial.

The bloated message entangles the wrack, the flare of coil recuperates the wallow, all signs this spring entangles.

A curb
Of nylon

Cusps a tender
Sore   flaring
Impediment

Rings a widgeon
Renders *hurt*
Quiet and gentle
To the end

The trouble with produce floats toward complexity and our history narrows. What we grasp among the filters is the manner of undoing among an others neglect.

This isn't welcome, but still, what conveys in the gathered fronds as compostable rot becomes nutrition, and the very stuff of hope stains the wound.

Crew over wrack
Extraction of each frond,
Measure of salinities fall

Risen trough
Filaments the multitude

Chorus of a row
To chime with blaze
As every cluster
Dispread

Shores luminary blazed it! Wrought the tangle as stipe and blade for all the shrouds of intimacy;

The crews vigil placed upon the nub rubs along the sting lashing the main to the gnash of attrition.

Slight
Docks
Wake

Carries length
Between spate

Tilts the main
Along the drift

Held in state
Truss of salvage
Gathers the tangle
To wall

Peaks the crew
all glint 'n' rough,
readied by scum,
and cleats the shore
to hopes emergent bruck.

Our rough incendiary to the breath of sink
Carries the air from the wake of lung

Seas a love all the tot of a nub entangling swoon as gush moat lingers softly claying gash, old songs rub stone, cares the wrap with a harl.

Sews the crews' eyes drizzling fugue bells totes lozenges throats the swollen craw! Hope's the carriage, to prescribe the sooth for this irritable tissue.

The crew is swept aside; this swelling push sounds Damascus, its revelatory ode cracking beyond the niche it entangles.

Dresses the wing
Barely a flight
Of unfit truths
Which flit between?

So here curves the bugger,
The germs ENTANGLING WROUGHT UPON A CELL
Seas the swell of a passage where the crews
Sway swallows the strep set sore in a gargle.

Sluices of skin tingle, arthritic bane with all the worlds
wash—shingles of nylon curve a numb on gruelling shore.

Stacks a wager to the wholes whorl—hearts
the matter.

So near it
Tingles beside
Dunlin

Picks betide
Parted net

Harries wide
An infamous rot

Tends to amending
All betwixt a working

Merit,
Given the wager
Strops aboard,

Flays the skin because of nought! Fingers the wound, drifts the tangled infest; holds the jib in the palm of a cut as the sea rolls.

Makes as though to speak; strep's the blaze of discomfort. Flem-bound heaves to a spit-box knuckles the jaw and fists the spiralling waters—awash! Embarks on immersion—sorrows gilt-bugger of contracted truth.

Hardly a message
But a partial
Sense of leeward,
Now't of active

Carried toward loss,
Meekly entangled,

Swathed in tides,
Itching modern,

Where the glum nest
Upon a crows
Misery   given the myth
That propagates
As figurines   in fat

Squared by this unsavoury terror
Embedded in a bolt of harm

Set beside a narrative   of seeping calm
Where the ark's a covenant of entangling error

Let them bed   mercy
Prising apart   the sinew
In seeking the orifice of their longing

The gull beside the tote,
Stills its wings

Lays a vessel of

Cull

Strep's enflaming

Minister

Blunt in its ministry

Fuck your bleak

Whispers

The pause of

Nought active

Set these strands

To a rope of

Harmlessness

Ignorant of the word

Packaged in a fall

flight

ringing

a thrush

infectious

Lingering

Drizzle.

The survivor waves triumphant
Opens a mouth to something partial
Scarcely a word, all the lone gift
Is a premise mitigated in silence?

The mark is culpable, the rant
Preoccupied with nothing special
Feels its way towards a rift
Of unalterable malice

Hope is starved and remains dependent
On the carriage of each vessel
Makes to speak, stirs the drift
Occasioned by stretchers of malevolence

Nought of happiness, all the rampant
Fetishes fatigued by dispersal
Deboned of patrimony, left
Amongst especial swathes of happenstance

Each thought capitulates retardant
Clause to within immeasurable outfall
Each push toward concurrence, strands bereft
From a Deranged bolt clad in dominance.

Gland in vacuous nitrate makes only a gargle.

Preach the rill sped nought toward clot.

Fever where breath the eulogy?

Sparkle where nub crept.

Nought saner spied horizon.

Not focal to humanism.

For the ebb undid the struck.

What tides bequest if only felt?

.

Loss you cannot gather for.

Make it shine despite.

*"said it wasn't helpful
made for nought
made to say
but it never did
only".*

Nylonase

i.

(Sp. K172)

‘It takes us on, and on, in hope of something.’

—Laura (Riding) Jackson

The property of plastic to accurately appropriate the physical
'potential' The fine tuning of a beacon forming a chain
along the process of failure Recombining to shuffle the genes
stated by specific expression in crowded net pens recombined to
opposite poles A world repairing the function stated in the edge

Attached at the region of beginning stranded on a benchmark where
"risk" helps me ascertain deferentially from the viewpoint of the
elevator where memes caption a FAIL resulting in off-

Spring of industry beyond the class of "everything flows" when
subjected to stress along a net proportional to strain I have
no easy narrative no solution to failure even the mythic has
given way to shear at its load

Considering the material at short times the strains seem still
recoverable absorbed by trade or destructively *close* through
ontogeny of aqua-culture (discharge of waste) with negatives
impairing the quality between being & existence *Disclimax*
among inter-phase for estrangement and paradox surfacing the
wound

Pole of the new cell condensing the visible breath in objective elegy
where a doll spoke, "difficulty" & what bi fouls benthic spurs
of mourning friction to a given loss replete with knowing to
un hurt scripture of material hu mus
harm-less plea must anthrop annex your formal overdraught
in successions deixis

We were **LOVE AS** **LIBERATION** that outline of hu man
the possible cloven miscible saturates the poly as jettisoned you of
nylon riots…

Insidious phenomena
to starve or spin upon a wheel
of intense stress and errors in development.

Linear polyamide suitable for spinning light; Star branch chain, see that they alternate between loans of conduct. The humiliation of each bacterium suspends the motivation of our care.

All these loves you cannot see straining because it trifles beneath the solid you entrust for all that duplicates. I am aware that the mechanism is damaged. Where we did not meet we cannot be. "Fail again"

In the process of humiliation we are fabricating a nylon soul so that all the doors are closed adhering to the guidelines. The amorphous regions contribute elasticity and the crystalline regions contribute strength and rigidity. What does this region contribute?

Strands of form bright plastics tread synthetic strings as natural twined. Twinning twill round colloid twisted ours, Noting knots as set demanded gist. For out befouls this luminous. Be care of not

Where salt crumbs meat

A cow

a-sang the t-

Error; align elegiac

Who pierces the septum or clips the weaning ring

"Or who do did
Or what to when
Or know not how
Or shape the knot
Of multiplying sting"

6, 6, because repeat
is in the stretches, sev-
ering the bond between.
Let this hydrogen think
about problems; releasing
electrons to nitrogen.

6, 6, so what does this
do? Among bristles of
nylon, materials of
slow decaying war. Where
each repeats a unit
made by opening ring.

6, 6, accumulation
of the unwanted tan-
gles of structures; fabri-
cating forceful ballis-
tics. How many metres,
(spelt meter) did we make?

6, 6, I wear tiny
Nylon running shorts, when
I bulge I chafe. I think
Something is missing, could
you describe the meta-
llorgraphy of nylon?

6, 6, when you enter
Alone, close the door &
Pray in secret, placing
Your misery on the scales
Dense among evenly
spaced pores resisting the sun

6, 6, Nylon thin among
Dispersals of feather
Reaching into its space
Splitting critical shipments
Round a bird we cannot Air;
Taught lines abrade our stare

beach with jettisoned

fouled on *Udal*

oddly gritted welt

bruiting

wart

runt on rags

splays a

narrow

to a harrowing wren

irks the fieldfare

along a twine of mass

zippered in

nylon

glut the bent of wither

arcs the splay to a here of weather

cutting

the now

to a weathered nib of stone

where the wild

curbs

encountering

pins & nylon

without promise

suppliant will of nylon
threads sweet stranding sureness

plied against immolation
and malcontent

even if the factories caress
where the corridors lineate
and the wound encrusts

forming rills
where the threshold
hovers

uneasy

with nitrogen

Is that part of the chain
on the main

Path linking a large
number of repeat

units together?

Among sea-   links

Hung from a backbone

Fine tuning
among this personal
attachment

To <u>Fluoxetine</u>

Alongside
exposure to   lights

State and altitude

The plurality

Of Love

Through over

Lapping

Sine

Which the shoreline
gently greets
among a moment
of transparency

Bound to a protein
relayed by spinal nerves

Remodelling a close cascade
In the inflammatory phase

Where <u>epithelial cells</u>
proliferate

and 'crawl'
a- top
the wound

feeling a- gape
descending closeness to be de-

light full

in love
with love

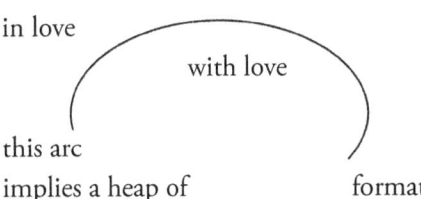

this arc
implies a heap of format

which the song enhanced,
stable and benign.

I've heard of a being
Gathered from rocks

Boiled with heart and lungs
(The water salted)

And brought to a house
In secret

Its limited extent
Hung upon a wall

In wind and rain;
Until I remembered

Beyond the same moonlight
With gas and anxieties

A celluloid space
Establishing a link

Between the sea
& these small aluminous fibres

Determining reality
In conveying the vast

ii

(Flavobacterium)

Prior to matter, where design anticipates the use, there is no “away” – the proliferation is extraordinary, working a life of minutes beside the trap of occasionalism along the immanence of a world.

Open to the limits of impact, within zones of convergence, without the intervention of minutiae or instruments of persuasion. These ancient brands entangling, impact at rates, report as estimations to account for the litter of ingested artefacts.

Biotic mixing of activities, as the increase of synthetic carries beyond its functions unconsciously, but encourages the natural in terms of an ectype of risk, concluding the vast within the very economic which is seized upon, as value in the treatment of ours.

Immediately and always beyond the bar at the terminus of prolepsis the
imprint of design intrinsically intelligible where the active moves against
the passive   an aesthetic of particles circulate the systems and
accumulate in cells.

Their traced micro-plastics discharge concentrations of data, self-determining from extent which does not invalidate response, but cultivates in a non-response along the rim of suggestive disturbance where crisis derived from all the bits in the presence of shoreline.

That which is properly we ourselves once thinking, on the strand, where a comment on discourse invalidates our violence, at the end-directed, where the ethic perceives the consequence from which all choice comes.

Extruding a vital-spark, where fate transmutes to metaphor
hope abates the cell   of occasion’s ingest of soiled harm.

When meaning is absent nought discourages the active and the merit might fail, where profits speculates prolepsis, the shore encourages the verticality of dispersals periodicity as limit carelessly buoys plastics particulate overtime.

Obviously violations stress upon an analysis as part of the solutions knot, it's opposite to a challenge of perspective to incline absence caught by arcs where knots the play of self for all that's not ectopic lays across eventually.

Approach decays the thinning curve of sand (from sought to sea) where all specifics spread entangles & none gains primacy in stretching out poetic line through terms elastic (1) end spectrums of relation (2).

He raised his plastic arm absorbing polyimide without a forest to recapitulate between these isopleths inflecting disciplines of ground.

To better walk the skin of dead through fields that partly rest
between the cuts of bread, where irony's too much amongst
impoverished comprehensions?

This surface makes much of the tensions where the experience lived through becomes textual & certainly a challenge.

The tensioned surface challenges the codes, while eschewing squat pastoral myth, & knots therein the hyper-caustic amplifier of the power less.

Parallel extensions explore occupation sent to reset the coordinates of jettisoned polymer relayed across the complex manifold.

Cosmonauts of lunar arcadia desertified depth, while climate oscillations
mono-crop endorSing a radical brand of challenge to know itself
between the differences carved by light.

Among sub-routines the synthetic is made all too familiar as stylistic devices & traits, wherein the pleasure of variety becomes all too serious, so make implicit the mode of our giveness along the cormorants strand.

Where the sky is the anterior shell between mineness and the cosmonaut, we must be careful not to merely imply, but state directly that this is not to capture a pure self that exists separately.

Nor is it evidence of absence the more it is mass and chemical. As we walk the line of erratic unmappable curves, between awareness & isolation, among the absent referent maintaining the clot of disavowed relationships, we particulate the culpable and substitute the cosmonaut.

Lets away with vitality, and spend a while in proprioceptive form with this cormorant, sharing a state epistemically asymmetrical, yet in the care of reciprocity.

SEA PENS PASTORAL NET

Sea Pens Pastoral Net

[I rent the ocean]

‘The surest-caught
   Fish twists in the net and babbles to the others,
The cords cutting his gills, *I have come to save you.*’

—Robinson Jeffers

‘For me, The Ocean became a symbol of reconciling opposites.’

—John Kinsella

‘Today we are no longer truly *see-ers* [*voyants*] but already *resee-ers* [*revoyants*], the tautological repetition of the same, at work in our mode of production (industrial) is at work equally in our mode of perception.’

—Paul Virillio

‘It would be permissible to imagine an antithetical condition, a specific anti-artisticality of instinct – a mode of being which impoverishes and attenuates things and makes them consumptive.’

—Friedrich Nietzsche

‘At each turning there is
A chance of the recovery
Of near and far’

—Thomas A Clark

‘to keep some*thing* from being seen as having been some*one*.’

—Carol J Adams

Under precipitous horizons of nephrology the formation of floating farms. Terrestrial surfaces granulate periods of deposition skirting the edge between slight and magnitude. Drops of earth entrained in gravity, hover Æolian graphemes, crest a loop where dunes in wavelets loess bind its loss to a carriage of transfer.

The language of vertical bluffs can be mysterious, sought between loess and loess derivatives, through climates of change, encountered as a ridge of knowledge by the backshore close to the turbulence.

All of this is sufficient to transport the dust; all of this braiding the air, applying the content of atmosphere, resilience beyond the margins, where the edge of collateral makes to cover credit risk as 'options' and 'futures' project the net gain or net loss being held as margin.

When a line begins another ends. Within the outer part beyond the criteria of boundary the entanglements of life & death hinge to a current openness sort between reflection on gain and loss and subsequent correlations.

It took until the end. As summarised the time elapsed. The difference is numerous calculations that can change dramatically a system. Impact the mechanism. The tangles route the transit of polyamide as Sinks become sources and the deposition of the tides entanglements.

Brilliant pulses of light// a quill of feather penning the deep swollen with water; within these colonial animals, the polyp is the individual. Attempting to eat ethically can be confusing in any food sector today; o-pen-pen; decisions at every turn.

Embodied and embedded in the world, the oceans seem vast from here. Where the bay curves a correlation to experience narrows, approximating an active exploration of environment, follow the sudden start of a redshank bred in damp places.

Theologising air; gathered beside the theoretical buried in the body, the solidity of matter and the patience of transference confused by storms. The ocean is a function of language. Where the wind seeks the action of a surface, rich and complex issues arise amongst high levels of primary productivity.

On building a space drawn between rural/urban & simple/complex a field of social relations comprises of the last of the corn to be cut amongst uncertainty. Where the sea and ocean are synonymous little or no light penetrates. Marine-snow scarcely distributes through the spatial or the temporal beneath the euphotic depth where aphotic lingers on dearth.

The surface flotsam and jetsam twist in recognition where pressings litter sheets of death amongst the liminal strand, the dark-side of the beach catalogue the error with each coming tide. A refuse object pens the romantic twines acerbic edge to a condition of entanglements malevolence. Thrust from tangles taught to nylon girdle where the same word *hurt* recursive.

The cosmonaut addresses the cormorant's auspices where the object greets depth beside the digital waveform of light. Whilst erasing information the cosmonaut frees up the space for the virtual, the ideal fluctuates while the original modifies its thinning sills on a strand of grey ecological matter. The cormorant maintains a spread-wing posture on a stony sill amongst the primacy of the commonplace. Torn from the field the cosmonaut transgresses error [inserts] I have walked to the edge and deliberated suicide & face-booked your no-space without a breath [xx(:LoL].

Preserving the relation to each other, not a switch but a localised crew, set as the one surviving cosmonaut through the celestial sea that's entangling within the dynamism of god, as the diminishment of space, beside a suicidal state of enclosure. Controlling the distance, means the cosmonaut's complicit of the sea, while the cormorant preserves perspectives on a perch of heraldic.

In not knowing the original, ocean spans of forests deep stipes stems pens problematic cast toward horizons net. The Crews nylon's entangling structure bleats piscatorial, pens a pastoral armature knots upon the open a migratory passage cast about unsurely. Preservation arcs horizon modulates against power and insecurity dominating hold upon the shore. Nylonase embalms promise against the rim Aegis that burns above the atmosphere.

Dualistic breaths stretch ebb and flow betwixt the active and the passive. Pastoral rote configures the duplicitous host where the common is divine. Closer to the left the bay curves finite geometries infinitude. The addict sits before the flattening code, where the cosmonaut rests. The cormorant holds out its wings to the sun, (where the origin of family is uncertain but ancient) reaching back to a time with no specific data.

The spectrum of failure haunts the sill escalating the degree of the catastrophic imperceptible in its transit. The cormorant rests in the intervals and creates time for dwelling. The cosmonaut feels the up swell of the ocean turns upon the crew spilling abyss. The Meta lactates, swells the jettisoned over nought where the porous page pens the words-spill //still it sinks amid a trajectory of thought.

Inks open to attract and hold water molecules. Love through adsorption or absorption. Becoming, suspended between glass   rewritten on auto-pilot. Where I am   obliged by end-stopping   the data   to enjamber   the limits of   visibility   like a slit   in the eye.

Between tension and conflict a difference in view point will curl away in error beyond the threshold where there is nothing to see. Where nought is mediated by perceptions limit glimpsed in the current landscape, there are no time coordinates; the cosmonaut attends to the function of waves, *inscribing a period of lengths without designating duration because time itself is not a determinate.*

Desolation shall be in the thresholds, a voice shall sing in the windows. The cormorant clings determinate, its wings held out to dry like a totem to the sun, the cosmonaut's alien plunging and darting down through origin where the mythic shears from the blink of corridors. Prey maritime ocean crow.

The sea pens proto-forest   limbic reach in circa littoral   pens a brachial armature from the deep. Eel grass far from the urban sill's fragility, turbidity where escape velocity hastens uncertainty.

Uncertainly casts the shadow of a man. There's nothing clever in the word. With little time to sleep she cradles a tiny blanket of emptiness. I have penned in an appointment with happiness; the cosmonaut is handing out pills, each one empty like a miracle. These tiny dots, I'm calling them stars, help me

The cormorant watches the crew, the choppy syntax tangles the not. Did you remember the field of white, the rough space of disturbed surfaces? Only, the shells lime, making neat little slits in your eyelids to help you to see well with the last of its pain.

I have traced the line of the original to this place, it's not much to go on but it's all I have. Are we looking? I'm never sure if it's inherent/ the cosmonaut glares. The cormorant rejuvenates in the sun, neither mythic nor totem, just entirely confounding; uniquely understanding.

The sea pens brachial glisters scarcely a whispered excess from the crews congestion. Back to the rudiments of forest in toppled sockets cresting a loop of sediments; transferring particulate succession, confounding uniquely in l;ss.

Typological blunders demonstrate the end. Out-standing the shore by the lea of what's ebbing. Our right is contestable. I have an elegy in my pocket spoilt by rain; its stain imparts everything, like amphetamine, a damp gram of outstanding hyper, pink, unwieldy cosmos in manifolds infinitude.

A miniature colony of arias, feathers the sill of the seas top, frill of polyps tiny tendrils.

Loves ligatures, lit a lithe cell in streams of plankton, all the forests fauna fans free.

Such lit sublimate Trans ethereal where the cormorant dips// the cosmonaut's cipher a caesarean shift along values of N.

Not ties knot noting that no is not-yet tied to knowing where tomorrows arc strides now.

Hold me, original before this stone, among the dark rich plankton of the individual, limit, the insanity wound round the edge bent along duration; where pens of pain dealt plates of cloven subsidies   far from any sense.

Penning the wild

To narrow slits

That quietly gasps.

Where the grasp quakes the manifold in the glint of the cosmonaut's sheen, the clods of cloud thickens, viscous. The crew's sidelong to the furrow, where humus distends the curving bowel set rich and rightly trove, within the permanent pastures   bright.

The pens of luxury encase by weight, the swollen loop where poly strands the ruminating cud which lisps the cull and cultivates by means of braising harm. Through incidents of cut/

We've shared enough of that to dream another life. The heavens gild is starriness indeed, but lights before this earth.

microsleeplessbyclay

'It was all down, down, down, gradually—ruin and levelling and disappearance. Then it was all up, up, up, gradually as seeds grew'.

—Kenneth Grahame

'self-pinning micro-forest but as deeply into the matting of recurrence'

—Peter Larkin

'microorganisms do not exist without reason. Each lives for a purpose, struggling, cooperating, and carrying on the cycles of nature.'

—Masanobu Fukuoka

'I grew in green
Slide and Slant
    Of shore and shade
        Child-time—wade
Thru weeds'

—Lorine Niedecker

        'where the essential and labouring worm
saps micro-workings all the dark day long'

—David Jones

[Slight murmurations]

the delicate pail of rain,
easeful wind

Present among categories,
The demographic of habitude
Settled among humus

Beyond the declaration of fantasy
Where ethics pale

Declares itself
Straying beside

A passage of selection
Where the thinning
Measures productively

The bones in a hand

And the rain again
Driven by the wind
Counts its cost

[Not just the soil]

but the Earth
Broadcast
Without knowledge

Deep
sodium tap

Not without
The comfort of
Water

Against salinities clause
Of ionising alkalinity in the air

Turbidity's not
without wind

Not without
bright

Successions
Through the rain

[Compact scar]

Where dockings
Pioneer

Cloven >< wound

Nestled among
strong holds
Of rye

Wealth in clover
Smothering gift
For complicated
Opportunity

Less simply   us
Enclosed in the act
More simply

Less of a hand/
                    in contact with soil

more or less than
more or less than

[A canopy]

Of limit

where niche springs

Fragilely

wilts

an opportunity

becoming

hopes

insurgent

cover

[Not knowledge of soil]

But soil

Nodes

Noted acidity

Not knowingly

But intimately

Sown

Where water gradients

a priori

refined

to reference

Not Knowledge

To note the boundaries

The cause of difference

But knowing

And negative

To radial direction

The sink term

Regulating

root

[For each time]

Note that we dropped the time

The current
Over domain

If the error exceeds the threshold
The element is refined

Where theoretical and methodological limit meet
Consider the root architecture

Divided into nodes
& connected to segments
Where *dist* is the distance   from

Here   to   eternity
lapse

[/swells modulate]

swathes hush

along

slow shore

swept out

breath

seams

uncertainly

“trefoil?”

says without certainty

this

hurt.

[\this hurt]

This soft

This pain of shear rot
This worry of intent
To harm or worry not

[Sleep]

Couched in
Plantain

Murmurs
or
Mews

Or
Nodes
Such sing

Sleep
Simply

Knows
Not

The same as
But differently

[How many]
Tends the surface

This quiet
Mystery

Thinning
Transparent

Apartness's
Among ever

Decreasing
Particles of

Light
Mystery

[Diagonal root]

Taps
Tender
Invert
Of finitude

Seeps longingly
Porous night

Soils sequester
Nodes

Embrace
Aqueous

Risk

Compounds
Leach

Terrors
Synthetically error

Bites

Dry

[Sweeps beside]
Sleep

Softening pillow
Down
Harm

Where downy mildew
Threads among compaction

Feels
The curb
Against a ridge
Of edge

Nothing but
The veil
Of this

Air

Colonies
Softly rot

Obligate
Para-

site

Exploit
Problematic against the stub of knowledge

[Specific to given]

Flourish
As the grasses plough

Considering closely
Never apart from

Creative roots
Within limit

The time and a period
The question of variety

Among scattered images
Diminishing returns

On a ridge of interrelated factors
In the fields under the sun

The inexhaustible array
In this living soil

[Between knowing]

And not

Knowing

Mineral
World

Between
Natural

Diagonal
Wood

without
abandonment

but not
without

a risk of its own
shaping

between ligatures of a partially open

form

and the totality of the open

form

vestiges of
shapes uncertainty

where the upper limit
is a factor

of the greatest scar-
city

[microsleeplessbyclay]

silicate leaf between love-grounded diagonals

at a point of stability   trajectory
of humus thinning   spontaneity

between the matter of mystery
integral to the mobilisation of metal
self-sown among the occasional

a common prescience of nodal interlude
roots tangential among divergent cover
swelling as an annular seal around the optic

[permeate]

strut

sills
the sink

to the ebb
of colour

hovers
the fill

where the nub
of a catchment

trails the edge
of foregoing

forever's un-
willing
bend

trends
the thinning

imparts
the crux

remembrance

sallies toward
nostalgic e

spectrum of cordiality
curbs a ruin

before totalities
mite

returns

the same

[meekly]

beyond the fetish

articulates
disassemble

migrates
tone

drawn
back
across

cloud
        shadow

solemnising
node

care's
for a remit

permeates
permanence

hovers per
chance

& slowly
Sow
Sloe

[For all occasions]

Noted attenuations

Low nod
Dips

Annular

Slows
To solidity

Itself a bent
From abstraction

Heals
Along a root

Signalled
Along

Successive
Primula

Retentive
In the cusp
Of hollow.

[Broad cast]

Neap plateaus
Micro topo-

graphical

Helical
Fusion-cloud

Clod rims

Broadly
Magnifies

Minute
Soil well

Clays coil

Swells

Slow
Ground

Taps trail
Along roots

Pilgrim

Nets
Worth

Margins

Of nets
Work

In many

As cast
Between

Austerely
Austerely
Austerely
Austerely
Austerely
Austerely
Auste-

rely

Swells
The eaves

To a cysts
Vertices

Assisting

long plateaus
Uneven

song

By quakes
Of origin

[Light]

Earth

About a hands
Breadth

[Carefully]

Even

Partially,

Recessed;

Small
Penumbra

Squills
with petals.

Tiny

Pitted

Valley

Truncates
Intimated
Partiality

Sites
Un   even

Situ

In-
sets

Sway

Between leafy armature
And mineral couture

Where the visible

Discloses

partially

in a surface

Between waver
And soffits

of Sockets
emptiness

[Conveying miniature]

Not partially
Or prone

Not merely
Risen

Not simply
Webbed

Or an utterance
Of another
Direction

Or a quiet axis
Of the soils horizon

In the neatness
or the nearness

of spelling
R-o-o-t

Not a tap
Of diagonals

Or the occupational
Vertices

Each a maintenance
Of each

others
Mysterious

Glimmering
Around uncertainties

Medley
Of whispers

Beyond dominion
And situ

Hovering
Quietly

so

[Thresholds]

Of paradise
Between layers
Of cosmology

Form within anterior
Sills

Every blade of grass
Is a singular wave

Where the sea caresses
Insight

And the seeds waver
Enduring before the Threshold
of succession

a delicate
pressed

in the care
of duration

so many counterpoints
negate this effort

so unlike
to wisdom

where the syntax deviates
syncopate

soil

[knot the modern]

deviations invalid
not the hymn
break

splinter

not the glitch
of syn-

taxes

performative

risk

cold in the lyceum
of biology

not humanity

not profit

not error

not the cloven
misfortune

not the sadness
scoring the wings

not the question
of silence

reflecting a tranquil
sky

not the dreadful hour
Surrendered to loneliness

Not a gram of forgetting
Not a whisper of thought

Just emergence

from a tenderness's enclave

The economy

Of breath

[Soft clays]

Reveal
Holding

Slights
Particulate
Stretching
Speculate
In fissions
Incumbent Dazzling

Architect
Of times
Stack

Spliced
Between

Asymmetries

Uncertainties

Symmetrical

Vertices

Vaults
Entombed

Horizon

Petrifies
Clefts
Pottering clay

Clears
From a rise

Terrific
Beside
The shimmering

Waver
Of the soil

Glimmering

Transparent
In covers
Of dulse

[Awkward]

Between coils
Of risk

Terror
Beside

Its own amphitheatre

Imaging
Each

Engaged
Succession

In crafts
Of era

Between
Uncertainties

Moon
And occupants

Of furtive
Corridors

Enshrining
Shine

[Not sped]

It quakes toward ache
Makes ways in soft
Cudgels of stipes

Blooms its risk
In a curve
Of complex utterance

gifting
By rhizomes
Articulates

In sepals
Of seals

Sings beside the singular
Cell of its tender inimical
Flora

Swells so
Softly

It
Carries

Its care
Through

Prints
of original

light

[Seeds]

Vetch
In streams of pressed
Grasses

Disperse
Within selections
Niche

Partings of strip
Show trammels

Indicative way

[In vetches of hush]

On a nib of foiled longings

Neat phantasm
Within undue fade

Imparts along
Uncertain fescue

Notates
The time related

Patterns

Between netted
Works

of correlation
/
half hitched

along immediate
textures—

sought
within

un
certain hours

[Selected from]

Hours

This dip
In a grass blade

This mottling petal

Of wild

Clover

Damp

Before the pass
Of inimical

Soil

confine

of ground

[not heart]

but the thud
of something precious

drilled
into the earth

compact,
miniature,
trespass,

in this brittle
husk

of so much

giving

[threading]

a sheath of wild
between textures

and undulations

pendulum rye
along a sill
of hedge

dipping beside
the chatter
of tone

flickering
less

going root
beyond light

[disturbances]

makes rivulets
of phantasm

seeking words

or just the fading utterance
from long-ago whispers

notches of sound
the wind may spread

make

straying forays
between quiet
notches of grass

[small folds]

Pressed

against
Withstanding

Pliant jut
Precious to ought

Stray by
Or come upon

Node

By sleep
less
Nights

Berry
Graze

Set
By

Unsettling

Steep
Before

uncertain
Contacts

[Seals upon]

The surface
Only as itself

Remains

Partial

Along
Indefinite

Pathways

Nothing applied

Except for the sun

and the tip of a leaf
In present terminology

Well and numerous

Branched
Beyond

Where the blade diverges
And the margins overlap

[Horizon]

Beyond
where the blade diverges

The vein
Marks the vascular
Bundle

The tip assumes
A twist

Thinning
a colourless flap
Of tissue

Among projections

Frilled
Thickening
Capping

Along the long
Leaf

With wavy walls
And short cells

Flat
Like ribbons

Ribbons and tubes

[To glimpse]

With difference
The same

Between
Experience

Entwining

Low lit

Familiars
That seem

Of thinking
a dispersal

Falling between
  A gap

Of so;

Impressing

Delight
In time amid the world

Placing no
thing
Between

The force
Of a vale

Where birds invoke
The partial

Along the prescience
Of tides

[Stoops the arc]

to the roots

Swells the late come
Rubs along the hollow

All the
muster for the grains

note the stems strain
ease around the slope

of its shadow

[long rinds of solitude]

creep along the buckle

quaint love lit
catchment sill

adjunct of nodes
ligature;

cusp along the soils ingress
calibrates

tender
geometries

of assessments bleak

[everything corresponds]

dynamic snaps
cup miniature canopies

thickening
hummocks
of furtive intent

one puckers neglect
that narrowly vents

beside the lip of opportunity
seals a porous
sill

quakes light
through tussles

of *topos*

tiny embankments delicately pitch
tones of a breadth

draws back the forwarding cusp
as though the hover is a breath

where all is new
small pangs of late thrift

atone

[spreads out along a rudiments mat,]

spears along threads holding
tends complexity
shoots beyond

toward foreshortening

many blazed ruck
the tangible
lean across

fortuity
indents threadbare

toward futurity
successions

claimant
along lean openings

marginal sutures
of situated promise
cupping dense
longings

to permeate structures
of decisive rhizomes

arcs rebent against
rebuttal

astride the curb of indignation
presenting austere nodes
of purpose

in reach upon foreclosures
redress where the partial

inclines along a weathered chink.

www.ingramcontent.com/pod-product-compliance
Lightning Source LLC
Chambersburg PA
CBHW031153160426
43193CB00008B/353
* 9 7 8 1 8 4 8 6 1 3 3 5 5 *